Survival Tips for the Pending Apocalypse

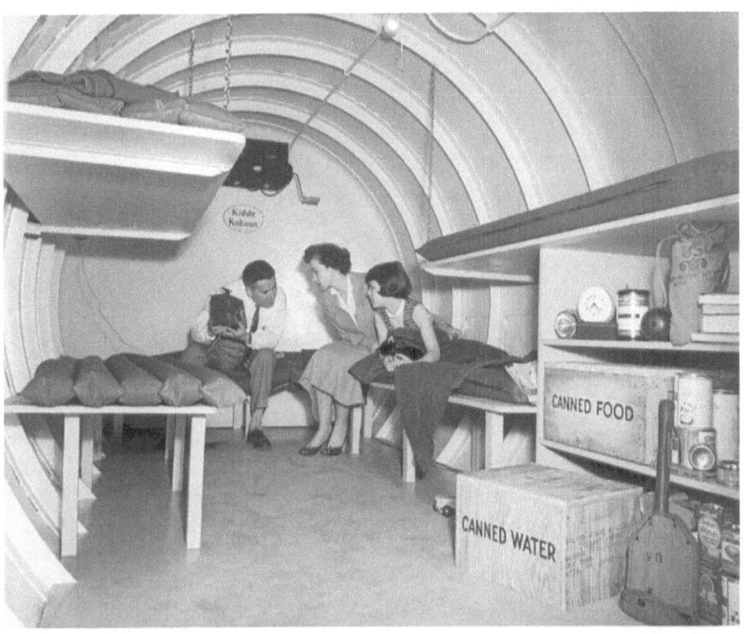

Poems by Shawn Pavey

Kansas City   Missouri

Spartan Press
Kansas City, MO
spartanpresskc.com

Copyright ©Shawn Pavey, 2019
First Edition 1 3 5 7 9 10 8 6 4 2
ISBN: 978-1-95038034-3
LCCN: 2019941990

Design, edits and layout: Naomi Pavey, Jason Ryberg
Cover image: Jay Halsey
Author photo: Naomi Pavey
All rights reserved. No part of this publication may be reproduced or transmitted in any form or by any means, electronic or mechanical, including photocopying, recording or by info retrieval system, without prior written permission from the author.

"Shawn Pavey digs deeper than almost any poet I have ever met. *Survival Tips For The Pending Apocalypse* is proof. He has planted a seed *while grasping at the impossibility of moments just passed.* He has written beyond the now. This is his *buckeye*. Hold it in your hand. It is *that fruit of immense/ wooden possibilities.* I know, one day, years from now, another poet will be *shaded by its branches and breathe oxygen from its leaves* the way I have. It brings me peace to know that feeling of salvation will continue to be spread."

—Huascar Medina, Kansas Poet Laureate 2019-2021

"Reading these poems I'm a little kid again, holding a green glass bottle to my eye like a telescope, seeing my world transformed through unexpected vessels: Buick LeSabres, bowling pins, Stratocasters, buckeyes, and barbecue grills. I'm on a rainbow arc from Cheap Trick to Unamuno. But the voice is Pavey's alone, singing a protest at times, singing flashes of transcendence, always returning to love of the grit and fall and rise of life."

—Nicole Sarrocco, author of *Ill-Mannered Ghosts*

"The opening poem to this collection knocked me out, and it hooked me on the book right away. I couldn't wait to read more, and I wasn't disappointed. Pavey's poems are both accessible and full of beautiful language. He has a sense of rhythm that can't be taught. His poetry is both particular and universal. I loved this book and highly recommend it."

—Daniel Crocker, author of *Leadwood*, editor of *Trailer Park Quarterly*

"Fellow travelers, open *Survival Tips for the Pending Apocalypse* and spoon your inner guide. After the hooking, Shawn Pavey gently pulls the barb from our lips knowing that when fishing for ghosts, the sweetest method is catch and release. He's not a poet who wants to lose you. Shawn Pavey is a poet who desperately wants you and his aching-aching voice to be found."

—Paul Koniecki, Associate Editor, *Thimble Literary Magazine*

"This poetry collection achieves that goal of finding *where the separate become singular / ...to be the one thing, whole*. The only way to balance out even some of our planet's horrors is to learn how to hope, laugh, love, and employ sarcasm whenever we need it to endure. If you need survival tips, Pavey's a good man to heed."

—Alarie Tennille, author of *Walking on the Moon*

"There is a persistence to time, a monotony to the moments that fill our lives like so many drops of water in an ocean that's ending. This, my friends, is where Shawn Pavey comes in. This book you hold in your hand reminds you that time is not linear, it is measured and conceived in our memories. This book reminds you that in the little deaths of boredom there are moments of such supreme beauty that we have to close our eyes for fear we might not want them to end. Shawn Pavey's *Survival Tips for the Pending Apocalypse* is a bar napkin elegy stained in whiskey. It's a prayer you read while gazing though cigarette smoke at the night sky, waiting to see if again the sun will indeed rise again."

—Jason Baldinger, Co-author of *Little Fires Hiding* (Kung Fu Treachery Press)

"Pavey takes us on a journey across the peaks and valleys of a life with this epic volume and shows the kind of companions which are there for a man every step of the way: women, whiskey, guitars, blues music, breakfast with friends at 4 am, and, of course, the blue Mustang. These poems sing of the bevy of jobs we need to make ends meet, the vulnerability of your last few bucks burning a hole in your pocket, the wholesomeness of coming home to a woman you love, the angst of a sickening political climate, and most showcase Pavey's real gift: his attention to the small details of the world. The details which come together to make the concert of a life."

—Jeanette Powers, author of *Sparkle Princess vs Suicidal Phoenix*

Earlier drafts of many of these poems appeared previously in *Talking to Shadows* (2008, Main Street Rag Publishing Company) and *Nobody Steals the Towels from a Motel 6* (2015, Spartan Press). Many of these poems have been published elsewhere over the years. The ones I can remember and/or document are:

Cold Afternoon, Dear Lucille , Story, Lament in the Key of 4G, Getting Away– *PresentMagazine.com*
Poem Starting With a Line From Phil Miller, Joel Explains Why My LeSabre Isn't Ready, God Is on His Way, Survival Tips for the Pending Apocalypse – *Rusty Truck*
Stunted Spring , Breakfast with Baldinger, Robert Johnson at the Crossroads– *The Gasconade Review*
Love Letter to the World, Meme Language Poem– *Winedrunk Sidewalk*
At the Waffle House – *The Charlotte Poetry Review*
Hollow Point – *Prompts: A Spontaneous Anthology*, West 39 Press and *Rusty Truck*
How to Keep a Fairy Down – *Recession in Neverland*, Paladin Knight Press
Thaw – *The Main Street Rag*
Leonid Meteor Shower With James – *The Blotter*
Architecture – *Cant*
Analysis – *The Kansas City Star*
Finding Zen in Cow Town – *PresentMagazine.com* and *Finding Zen in Cow Town: An Anthology of Poems About Kansas City*, Spartan Press
Listening: an excerpt from *To the Stars through Difficulty: A Kansas Renga* – Mammoth Publications

TABLE OF CONTENTS

Acknowledgements
Foreword by Mike James

Section I

Autobiography / 1
A Letter to My Elders / 8
Catch and Release / 10
Twin Sisters, 1981 / 12
Stumbling / 13
Discarding You / 15
Still Life in Water: Pamlico Sound, July, 1987 / 17
On Eastway and The Plaza / 18
I Drive to Late Autumn, 1980 / 20
Intangible / 21
Cold Afternoon / 22
What I Say to You After Work: for Naomi / 24
It's Late or Maybe Early / 25
In My Dream With Bruce Springsteen and
    Steven Van Zandt / 27
Limited Vision / 28
Poem Starting With a Line From Phil Miller / 30

Section II

Talking to Shadows / 32
Unemployment / 34
Healing / 35
Waking the Dead / 36

A Poet Working as a Hotel Night Auditor / 38
September 24th, Overland Park, KS / 39
My Radiator Runneth Over / 40
Joel Explains Why My LeSabre Isn't Ready / 41
Reclaiming the Light / 42
Monday Morning, 6:45 a.m. / 44
Avoiding Traffic on the Morning Commute / 45
Turning 45 / 46
Stunted Spring / 48

Section III

Little Big Star: for Alex Chilton (1950 – 2010) / 50
Dear Lucille / 51
Thermodynamics / 52
Poem for Sara Romweber / 54
Excerpt from *Ghosts on Water: A Kansas City Reng*a / 56
The World is Small and Fragile Still / 57
Remembering / 58
Love Letter to the World / 60
Breakfast with Baldinger / 62
Robert Johnson at the Crossroads / 63
A Gift, So It Seems / 65
Auditioning for Heaven / 66
Schizophrenia / 67
Jason Ryberg in the Gasconade / 68
Tapestry / 70
At the Waffle House / 71

Section IV

Story / 74
A Christmas Wish / 75
Ignoring the Homeless Man at the Corner of Johnson
    and Antioch, Then Meeting His Eyes / 82
Crossing the Street / 84
God Is on His Way / 86
Lament in the Key of 4G / 87
Getting Away / 88
Hollow Point / 89
Meme Language Poem / 91
How to Keep a Fairy Down / 92
Survival Tips for the Pending Apocalypse / 93

Section V

A Bluesman's Guide to Eastern Religion / 96
Rumbling Through Dreams / 97
Thaw / 100
Leonid Meteor Shower with James / 101
Modern Alchemy / 105
Morning / 106
Excerpt from *Radio Renga for KKFI* / 109
Manifesto No. 132 / 110
Architecture / 111
Homecoming / 112
Analysis / 113
Inaudible Song / 115

Soundproof / 116
Tread Marks on Mars / 117
Ladder to the Moon / 118
The Planets / 119
Finding Zen in Cow Town / 122
The Last Lunar Eclipse of the Millennium / 124
Dissonance, Late August / 125
Entertaining Equilibrium / 126
Eagle Landing / 128
Listening / 130
Tempus Fugue / 131

There are so many people to thank in a collection like this. This book contains more than three decades of work, so I'll start with the teachers who gave me enough encouragement to keep at it: Dan Simmons (yes, *that* Dan Simmons), Marcie Poncelow, Vicki Huneycutt, Sharon Barringer, Chuck Sullivan, Dr. Robert Kirkpatrick, and Dr. William Harmon. Of course, I need to thank my parents, Keith and Barbara Pavey, who (at least not to my face) never retreated in horror at the suggestion that I wanted to write poetry. I'd like to thank my brother, Eric, for always having my back. I extend hearty thanks to M. Scott Douglass, Jason Ryberg, and Will Leathem for publishing my books. My wife, Naomi Pavey, is the best damned copy editor I know and a patient and wise woman. Jay Halsey is a talented writer, exceptional photographer, and dear friend who shot the cover photo for this book. Finally, there are so many poetry and art friends whose support and love kept me going after it for all these years: Chuck Sullivan (again), M. Scott Douglass (again), Tyler Riggs, John Dorsey, Mike James, Maryfrances Wagner, Greg Field, Brandon Whitehead, Jeanette Powers, Jason Baldinger, Scott Silsbe, Paul Koniecki, Huascar Medina, James Baxter, Nicole Sarrocco, José Faus, Alarie Tennille, George Wallace, Daniel Crocker, David Childers, John Burroughs, Diane Borsenik, Al Ortolani, Stef Russell, Scot Young, and Kevin Peery. This list could go on for many more pages. If I left you out, I'm picking up the bar tab next time.

-SP

Shawn Pavey's Blues

This is a big book. It's big in the literal sense because it's longer than most poetry collections and it's big in the metaphorical sense because it covers a large selection of fine work from someone who has been writing well, without tenure or grants or accolades, for a few decades now.

Survival Tips for the Pending Apocalypse starts off with a nod to the past. The first poem *Autobiography,* is both an homage to that most long-lived of the Beat poets, Lawrence Ferlinghetti, and a recounting of Pavey's life. Over several image-laden and fluid pages he moves in and out of time and surrealism. Along the way he comments on what he sees as *The writing/ on the wall writes itself these days. /Kilroy got that vacation he wanted/all this time. I think he took his dog.*

One of the thousand ways *Autobiography* works is through the wistfulness Pavey employs. As a poet he is always about four steps away from breaking into tears. Pavey turns almost every poem into an elegy. He is always mourning what passes: his childhood, his loves, his friends, or the stupidity of what men do to one another.

Musicians are referenced throughout this book and it is clear Pavey knows the blues. He knows the blues are not just about sadness. The blues are about being alive and knowing life is transitory. There's joy in sitting in a parked car listening to the last bit of a Springsteen song. And that joy can't exist without sadness. Pavey gets that too and the sadness is there when the song ends and Pavey's speaker gets out of his car and faces another office day.

As far as the blues, Pavey has written the best poem ever written about a blues legend. That only sounds like hyperbole until you read *Robert Johnson at the Crossroads*. Then it sounds like obvious fact. The poem is so successful because it's offered as a strict bit of anecdotal narrative. There's not a metaphor or simile anywhere in it and the language is so stripped down it could have come right out of an old blues song. Since Pavey trusts his readers, he isn't afraid to allow them the imaginative space to color in the lines he drew.

There are so many well-drawn lines in this collection. And so many quotable ones, too. It's easy to make a list of favorites. Every reader will have a long list.

—Mike James, author of *Jumping Drawbridges in Technicolor,*
First-Hand Accounts from Made Up Places,
and *Crows in the Jukebox.*

For my wife, Naomi, who understands when I rise from bed after midnight to scribble.

Section I

*Remember the sky that you were born under,
know each of the star's stories.*

—Joy Harjo

Autobiography: *after Lawrence Ferlinghetti*

I am leading a quiet life in
my place every day
watching a pride of
domesticated lions fight for
no good damned reason. I
am leading a quiet life on
Outlook Street in Mission,
Kansas, half a continent
away from the town where I
was born in Maryland,
north of DC.
I am an American.
I am white and in the middle
class. I am middle-aged and soft
around the middle in the middle
of America. I am fair to middlin',
as my granddad would say. I have
no right to write about race but I should
listen and listen and listen
and really hear. I was an
American boy. I flunked
out of Cub Scouts in the
suburbs. I thought I was Han Solo
staring at stars on my back in the
Great Plains dreaming of

piloting spaceships. I had a baseball mitt but couldn't catch. My Huffy 10-speed took me out of the driveway and on to the gridded streets of Longmont, Colorado, where I rode over every inch of that town and further still to Lyons and across the Foothills Highway to Boulder and then the flat ride home. I delivered the *Daily Times-Call* at 4 in the afternoon and 5 in the morning on weekends. How gray the ink stained my hands, how strong the newsprint scented my clothes, how heavy the weight of the papers I carried as I left our front porch, and how light I felt on the walk home. How that was work and I came to know it young. I had an unhappy childhood, yet it is hard to remember mixed with the splendor of aspen leaves. I watched rockets on TV and built my own to launch on the football field. I never got caught

stealing. I laid sewer pipe in
North Carolina summers for
$4.75 an hour to pay for college.
I went to college where Thomas
Wolfe did and when I look
homeward I don't know
what direction to face. I attended
three different schools by the
time I turned seven. I served in
no army and saw no combat. I
worked third shift at a Hilton in
Charlotte. I stayed awake all
night to balance accounts and
plunge toilets. I protested
the Gulf War in Lafayette Park.
George Bush did not notice me.
I marched from the White
House to the Capitol steps and at
day's end slept at
a Hilton because the
room was free. I marched in
parades carrying a big bass
drum behind the farting trumpeters.
I am rereading
The Portrait of the Artist as a Young Man
and my Facebook newsfeed. I am
watching the Kansas City Royals play in
the World Series for the second year in a

row. I have heard the Ginsberg Address
and the Victor Smith Address. I like it
here and I won't go back where I came
from because I cannot decide where that is.
I too have ridden airlines buslines trainlines
and travelled among unknown
men and women and never once
not been in America.
I read the Bible but doubt the flood.
I don't know where I was
when Rome was built.
I have been an ass.
I have kissed a girl
in a rainstorm and made love
in an ocean and watched
a sunrise from a mountaintop
completely alone. I
have wandered lonely in a crowd.
I am leading a quiet life in my
place every day watching
trees change clothes after
dyeing them crimson. I have
never set out to walk around
the world but I have run for
miles and keep thinking
about doing it again.
Room weary
I stress
I have unraveled.

I have seen Funky Town.
I have seen the crass mess.
I have heard Stevie Ray Vaughan
render. I have heard guitars teach. I
have heard Tom Waits in Saint Louis.
I slept in a starred hotel in Times
Square and in a flea trap in Denver and
I know why nobody steals the towels
from a Motel 6. I am leading a quiet life
in my place every day reading
résumés résumés résumés
trying to fill jobs so
rich men can make
money money money
telling machines to tell
people what to do.
I am the Classifieds section.
I sell a dream and I take my
cut. My office is at the
crossroads. I see another war is
coming and I see we have not
finished the last three. The writing
on the wall writes itself these days.
Kilroy got that vacation he wanted
all this time. I think he took his dog.
I stick to the alleys, the streets
are not safe. They took away
all the Plymouths, the
Oldsmobiles, the Pontiacs, too.

What is a man to drive these days? I
have driven the interstates and crossed the Continental
Divide and wallowed in the
woods of Chapel Hill rebuilding a life. I
saw the towers fall on television when I
was unemployed and broke.
I had a bad feeling.
It lasted eight years.
I am too goddamned young to die.
I moved to Kansas City for a
woman who did not want me. I stayed
and found one who does more days than not.
I am leading a quiet life in my place
every day contemplating
futility and joy. I am a part
of the world's quick decline. I
have stared at night
skies in pastures and through trees.
I have written
poems that I have
burned. I have
leaned in drunken
doorways. I have
sat on rocks. I have
suffered and I have
loved and I have
sung at full voice all the words
to *I Want You to Want Me*. I have
seen the paintings of

the Wyeths and Warhol, Rothko, Stanton
MacDonald-Wright, Jackson Pollack and Frida Kahlo,
Caravaggio, a Rodin
sculpture of a hand thrusting
out of a rip in space. I have
seen them.
I am a man.
I am leading a quiet life
in my place every day, mowing
the lawn and watching leaves change. I will
be there when the last
leaf falls this year and it
will mean something that I will
write down and scratch out
for being trite. I will
rake the leaves with Donald Hall
and have a talk with whatever happens next
in its dark and tattered robes
and ask it for a favor
you know,
just for me,
to take its fucking time.

A Letter to My Elders

All of you,

There was nothing to prepare me for this. I don't know why you didn't tell me about the world and how I can believe so hard in how everything should be and it just never is that, is it? I sit here at the beginning of my 45th year and I am no closer to understanding how to make it all work. I suppose this was one of those lessons I had to learn on my own. I get it. Really, I do. But a warning was out of the question? Was all that loving and hurting and loving and hurting necessary? Must the heartbreak accompany the heartfelt? And the heart; so fragile? Must it be so capable of complete shattering, so much so that the pieces never fit back together just right again? Will it always be this clunky, odd-fitting thing? You got the clichés right, I'll give you that. The world is an oyster. Such a slimy, messy, stinky thing. Hard to get at, hard to hold, smelling of salt and rot. So, yes, turning 45 and I'm still surprised by the struggle. But – and here is where it is all so brilliant – I'm 45 and still surprised by the surprise of it all, the joys of new joy, how the warm body of a lover in the night shakes away the hollow ache, how her smile washes away the shame and guilt and tiredness. All I want in the world is that smile, that body near me, that tender touch of the hand. And the laughing. Oh god, the laughing. You didn't tell me it could be like this. The beauty of a mountain stream, the triumph of architecture, Gershwin, The Ramones, Keats – each day there is that promise. Like today, finding music I'd forgotten I owned striking something in me that pulled these words out of my head. That these days follow dark ones, that writing happens and some of it may be beautiful, but there is always something there waiting to come out even when I forget how to listen for it. And that's the thing, isn't it? This is mine, this life. It's mine. Thanks for that. For this.

       Much love,

       S.

Catch and Release

Casting in rhythmic, smooth-measured motions,
he waits for a perfect moment to release
clear three-pound test, fluorescent yellow leader,
and a wet fly tied to the end of his line.

He pulls enough slack from his reel to make distance
and casts once more before he lets fly
an arcing line through clear mountain air
from the tip of his handmade bamboo fly rod.

The stone fly nymph he tied splashes down
slightly upstream of the pool by the boulder
on the other side of the river by the bank,
where he just knows deep in his angler's heart
a fire-bellied trout swims cool and patient
waiting for morsels to float by overhead.

His deception, skillful and knotted, hooks it
and pulls the rainbow into crisp morning light.
He feels it twist and pull and fight,
bamboo stresses and bends in hand,
his left deftly pulls line through the guides.

It splashes once more out of the water,
its tail flapping wildly to swim in the sky

as sunlight flashes on its slick, color dappled side
and sinks again into the churning stream
where my father's net waits to scoop it out.

Trying to breath the air that will kill it,
the rainbow thrashes in the net
as my father takes it in his hands,
puts his thumb in the fish's mouth,
and gently pulls the barb from its lip.

He places it back in the cold river water,
holds it, lets it readjust, makes sure it is strong,
and watches it swim slowly free.

He turned to me, water rippling in his wake,
and whispered a soft hook that caught me
even though I couldn't hear,
bubbling over the sounds of flowing water,
the words his lips mouthed like prayers.

I smiled at his smile, turned away,
and with smooth-measured motions
learned from his hands,
I cast my own line.

Twin Sisters, 1981

Imagine a mountain in Colorado in black night of early morning, late July. I am a teenage boy. Imagine a spray of stars.

At the summit, above timberline where trees cannot grow. A boulder, hollowed from wind and rain, heat and ice. Imagine I sit inside the rock, look down on rivers and lakes collected in hollows carved by glaciers through time. Sun crests the eastern horizon. Imagine flame. Imagine sky. Imagine reflections of sunrise mirrored on water thousands of feet below.

In that place and that time. I am small, and immense, all things and nothing. The only sounds: wind, breath, the beating of a 14-year-old heart.

Stumbling

I should have outgrown cursing
digital alarm clocks
stabbing me in dark warm sleep next to you,
waking me to rise
into the cold blackness of hardwood under my feet.

It is a dance with dread, this search by touch
through passion's shed clothes
for just anything to cover my skin
on the January stumble
to the white tiled bathroom floor.

Water steams and bounces off this skin
that only minutes before touched yours
and the feel of you burns through water
into my brain where it will stay all day
never letting fully go,

while I scrub then dry then shave then dress
and wrap a noose around my neck
and before slipping into my coat, you slip around me
and softly kiss my throat

and sacred unsacred rituals of doing the job
mean nothing as I stare at the clock

counting its ticks and tocks
as the hour's component parts
reassemble into one whole longing
that never goes away.

Discarding You

You walked alone outside
in the rain, splashing in and out of puddles –
no umbrella or raincoat – getting soaked.
Cold, you undressed
on the back porch, leaving soggy shoes
under a wicker rocking chair.

I would sit alone in that chair
watching you lie by the side
of the house that rarely sees any shade, your shoes
sitting on steps in front of me, bare feet playing in puddles
of light through elm branches, your dress
skirting up around your thighs, sun-soaking.

And Sunday mornings, each of us soaked
in lazy relaxation finding a chair
to read newspapers, dressed
only partly; covered, but barely. The side
of your face hidden in shadow as jazz puddled
in the air like incense. We wore socks, not shoes.

At the back door this morning, our old Irish setter shooed
flies away with his tail while pots soaked
in foamy dishwater puddles.

Wind rocked the wicker chair
and cigarette smoke drifted inside
the kitchen while I stood at the door half dressed.

Mornings, I dress and redress –
having become colorblind – matching shoes
but rarely socks, looking at my every side
in the mirror, blue and black always soaking
each into each other. Dirty shirts drape over chairs,
clean ones, rarely ironed, lay gathered in random
puddles.

All that is left of you here are puddles
of memory – every scarf, every dress,
every thread you ever wore bleeds together. And
your chair
is so empty now. The only scattered shoes
I see are mine. Soaking
wet, I stood alone in the rain last night, no lights on
inside.

Tonight, again, the rain resides in trashcan puddles
soaking though your dress
and the shoes I found in a bag behind your chair.

Still Life in Water: Pamlico Sound, July, 1987

when we swam away from the pier to where we couldn't be
seen from the shore our toes touched shallow coastal shelf
I held you by your slim waist fierce sun reddened our faces
our shoulders our backs our skin beaded water under that
wide blue sky each in that water each in that life each in
this memory I hold while the Pamlico flows to the sea.

On Eastway and The Plaza

Strip mall carnival's neon lights lit up the night
in mystical swirlings and spinnings and turnings
hurling bodies through cool autumn space
in the parking lot
next to the abandoned Cinema Blue.

Stopping at a light of different time,
popcorn, cotton candy,
pungent manure, and musky hay
so real in my nostrils' memory
I swear I could almost feel her
teenage warmth pressing so close to me
I could smell her hair
in the autumnal crispness of a September evening's
county fair air.

Walking hand in hand past
hoarse-throated barkers shouting
us into fraudulent pursuits
of nailing nailed-down bowling pins.
I spent my dollars taking away nothing
more than failure and shame in the innocence
of not knowing the scam.

Stopping off on the drive home
at an empty field,
we steamed windows in my father's Dodge,
revealing our awareness of tension,
of wanting,
of midnight curfews and lack of time,
of cool fall night breezes,
and saying goodnight
just short of it being fully that.

This stoplight changes its glow from red to green
and I ease my Mustang's accelerator down
leaving behind night's carnival light
in the fumes of my exhaust,
take the last cigarette drag
and flick the butt out the window,
heading through the streetlight darkness
towards home.

I Drive to Late Autumn, 1980

I drop a worn needle to a fresh groove as
Don't Stand So Close to Me twinkles
into the cans of my Nova 40 headphones.
Here, vinyl gleams its petroleum rainbow
smelling of paradise.

I am 13 years old. I am 13 years old
daydreaming of stage lights, guitars,
microphones, and the chance that doe-
eyed Denise Rodriguez bounces in the
front row of my rock stardom with her
long curly hair, exquisite silk skin.
She is everything lovely.
I sing to her and she adores me.

And now, gray-whiskered and 45,
driving a sedan on my way
back to work after lunch, I chant
Zenyattà Mondatta
Zenyattà Mondatta
Zenyattà Mondatta.

Intangible

I've written these poems a thousand times
in the air, watching as words drift without weight
into ether, into breeze and wind,
misting effortlessly away,
diffused, breathless.

I wish I could tell you these poems,
wish beyond wishing I could whisper
them in your ear,
smell you close to me, breathe you in.

That would be the poem I would write.

That would be the poem I would write
but it wisps away before I catch hold

and all I can do is stand by the garden,
jalapenos and tomatoes ripening into fruit,
watching poems float above them,
into them,

those words meant for you,
no paper to catch them, no pen to give them form.

Cold Afternoon

snowfall makes no noise,
falls as forgetting falls,
flake after flake.

—Miguel de Unamuno, *The Snowfall Is So Silent* as translated by Robert Bly

We imagine ourselves atmospheric,
waiting for a thick covering
of snow that we know will come. I
build a fire.

We blanket ourselves before it, fill
our space with warmth – these
rooms from which we will see
white flakes fall from gray sky

through cold glass of windows shut tight
against Kansas wind that seems to seep, still,
through cracks and seams around frames,
under doors.

It is like this in winter. It is like this
when skin shivers at the touch of air
colder than water frozen in the ground.

We settle in, adjust to walls familiar and
worn, to furniture that holds our shape, to
the warmth of our blanketed bodies. The
tea kettle whistles,

steams the windows. Outside, we could see
our breath and imagine ourselves as storm
clouds shedding snow crystals over
stubbled plains,

as snow clinging to bare branches of
maples, to needles and cones of pines,
coating browning lawns, covering sidewalks
and streets.

We imagine quiet and imagine snow,
imagine a day spent bundled up in the
warmth of each other, hastening that
which we know will come.

What I Say to You After Work: *for Naomi*

It's just a bad day, Darlin.
There have been others before this
and we're still here, still breathing, still
waking up in the morning to do it all over again.
I know. I know it has to get better. It will.
Let's go for a walk
and look at the maples in our neighborhood
budding their fresh green leaves,
shedding the whirlygigs
with their veined helicopter wings.
Let's feel the warming spring Kansas breeze
on our faces, let it tousle our hair
like a busy mother's touch.
Let's leave the smart phones
and music players at home.
Let's talk out the frustrations
and the humiliations and the fuckups.
Let's talk about planting flowers and tomatoes,
playing guitars, grilling, inviting friends over,
getting out of the house. Let's stop at the corner where
the redbud ignites against the greening grass. Let's curse
the dandelions but enjoy the yellow.
Let's give the bad day the attention it deserves,
which, really,

ain't much.

It's Late or Maybe Early

Finding myself unsleeping,
I stumble down stairs in the dark
while she sleeps soundly
tucked into our big bed.

I creak every creaking board
in this 60 year-old house
to my office/disaster of clutter,
pondering some noodling time

on a guitar or on a screen.
I don't plug them in, the guitars, not now,
not this long after midnight when
she sleeps, the cats sleep.

I listen to these Kansas winds
blow brittle branches off our
silver maple trees rippling
through new leaves outside my window.

The lawn could use a mow in a day or two,
but tomatoes and peppers ripen from the loam
in our backyard raised box gardens.
I love that, this growing of vegetables and herbs
on a lot so covered with trees

that there is insufficient light for anything
more than a couple handfuls of food
that squirrels and rabbits
don't eat first.

The air conditioner groans
against Kansas August,
even now, six hours past sunset,
maybe four hours from sunrise.
I leave the guitars on their stands,
stare at the lines of this poem
which I will revise and finish a year from now
and think that maybe, maybe now,
if I close my eyes sleep will come,
knowing that, even if it does,

tomorrow will be another long, bleary day.

In My Dream With Bruce Springsteen and Steven Van Zandt

There I was, sandwiched on a love seat
in a coffee shop between
The Boss and Little Steven like it was a thing,
something that happened.
I asked them how long they'd be in town.
I invited Bruce to a poetry reading.
He said he'd try to make it and I believed him.
I showed Steven my guitars.
We walked down the stairs to my basement
(which, apparently, is under the coffee shop).
Steven brought my beat-up Stratocaster with him.
The lights didn't work. Spider webs covered everything.
We swept webs and spiders away with a broom until we
found a functioning light switch. We took my guitar
apart together and Steven showed me how to swap out
the pickups. Bruce gave me soldering tips, screwed the
back plate back on. Emerging from sleep, I looked
around my storm-darkened bedroom as Naomi
showered for work.
The cats wanted food. It was Thursday.

Limited Vision: *with apologies to Dylan Thomas*

In the land of the blind,
the one-eyed man is king
—Tom Waits

Sounding not at all a going gentle,
wind and rain pound a sliding glass door
overlooking a night-blackened sea beating
ancient fluid rhythms frothing white
against a blacker shore.

There is no good night, my friend.

Screaming at the dark
of a new millennium's uncertain risk
of remaining human, of staying sane,
we cannot find our heads or tails
when madness tears at the envelope of our skull.

There are no good nights.

Not when days bring only what days will bring,
working ourselves into a stupor to make it all work,
exhausted from the strain.

Lost in the emptiness of what we perceive
of our senses relaying little sense,
in this disarming rage
we think too much,
we drink too much,
and pray
once and for all for just
that corner-of-the-eye glance
past the face of immutable blindness.

Poem Starting With a Line From Phil Miller

And the Adam's apple, the vocal chords and tongue,
the crackling voice graveled by whiskey, cigarettes,
and time cannot sing the songs, written so long
ago, now. That stage in the back of the bar? Empty.
That band so distant and estranged for all these years.
Guitars lie in their cases, gather dust on stands.
The record, somewhere, buried deep in a box,
its vinyl molding and warped, filled with dreams
that lie etched in grooves. Place it on a turntable
and listen as a needle fizzes in a rotary
swooshswooshswoosh and a lost voice barely whispers,
So young so young so young.

Section II

An enormous wreck of a bird
Closed on my heart in the darkness
And sank into sleep as it shivered.
                    —Galway Kinnell

Talking to Shadows

At times it hits me smack in the heart of my head
how the struggle to find the words seems so pointless
so endless so meaningless
when that strange magic I'm supposed to know
never quite manifests itself in *my* self
but rather strikes me so completely down
when I'm not ever even looking
at anything at all in particular
and the particles of a poem
escape me and leave me gasping and grasping
for intangible gossamer things
the dragonfly wings beating a blur I can't even see
but I hear the buzzing in my skull
of a disquiet I cannot name nor ever will
buzzing and flitting about my brain
these words these thoughts these voices of words
dancing a spasmodic dervish
whirling and spinning in self-flagellations and letters
and words and poetry dripping from my cells
my fingers my tongue and the beating of beating
dragonfly wings brings me no meaning
no meaning only names and names and nomenclatures
beating like wings in my brain
beating like wings without connections
without homes without places even to sleep

in those hours after witching hour
so I bitch and I bitch
when it's all too much the TV
is never enough every time
but nothing changes
the pain remains my pain and I keep it in a place
become unsafe where walls fall
bit by crumbling bit piling emotional composts
heaped in dark corners of decay
the deepest places I know
where I ask great questions of *Why*
and I find no answers where there are no answers
and don't you ever answer
don't you ever try
and don't you tell me
don't you tell me that
don't you ever tell me that the Shadow knows
because the Shadow don't know shit, man,
the Shadow don't know shit.

Unemployment

These days mornings find me in bed
a dragon dragging itself out of its gold
out of a lack of anything better to do.

It's a different day from yesterday
but yesterday was the same as the day before
in a way I'd rather not repeat today.

Clock radio alarms remind you
you can't always get what you want.

You never get what you want,
you only take what you can get.
The day after the day after the day after
yields only the linear monotony of time
passed getting out from under safe blankets of dream

when aren't dreams all we ever really want?

Healing

This bed becomes too big for me
lying awake in some sick-hearted stab at sleep
that rarely comes barely conscious
of a name being whispered
by a part of me still expecting
a quiet stirring of her slumbered reply.

I tried to cure this space with words,
dark-hour tossings pained by sharp corners of books
in my ribs offering no solace
save a solitary waking
when we all come to know all that we will ever know,
when the connections we fight to make fall short,
when no matter how hard we sweat
to be part of some other body,
we know we only ever are
the connected parts of our own.

A sun will rise and set in time
and we can enjoy that too
even if the measure of it seems too much
to take in all at once;

colors of emblazoned skies will not diminish
when loneliness puts you in a bed
too big, alone.

Waking the Dead

Nocturnal roamings ramble me about
my tiny unkempt borrowed room
when it gets too dark too quiet too still
and there's nobody to call at 3 a.m.
nobody at all and doubts scream out
in my skull leaving no room
for answers nor affirmations
or why I'm stuck in a chair chain-smoking cigarettes
when my throat is raw and the only voices I hear
ooze out of the pieced-together stereo in the corner
spitting through its transistors an analog past
struggling through a recorded distance
so black and empty
that it reminds me of nights like these

and it's always nights like these

that pull out what I've hidden in crypts
buried so deep I'd almost forgotten the rot
and the hollow cold ache in my chest
weighted by a cast-iron wicked January mass

and the desire to scream and rage and cry out
at the dark that wraps itself around me
with slimy wet blankets

comes out a constricted gurgle
of tempestuous crashings and thrashings choked off
just south of my throat
and I just stare at the ceiling
with all its cracks and stains
and the digital radio alarm clock
bleeds out into the dark
its red corpuscle numbers reminding me of a time
I'd just rather not even know
so I just yawn and change the tape
and think about sleep in a passing fit
of attempting the impossible
and decide to watch the sun come up in silence
and switch the stereo power knob to OFF
musing to myself that we vampires
still have so much to learn from light.

A Poet Working as a Hotel Night Auditor

might say he hated his job,
disliked numbers and the manipulations he performed
on them
like some perverted bookkeeper with a figure fetish
spending most of the night just trying to get off

and maybe has been heard complaining
about the whole mess his career has become
since graduating from college
at the beginning of a recession
with a degree in English

*I mean, Jesus, we all speak it already, why the hell did
you get a degree in it? Whadda ya wanna do, teach?*

but there really is nothing like unlimited access
to free coffee and staying
up all damned night reading books
after all the numbers have been wrestled and beaten
into compliance with the very idea of balance

which he never truly understood
and, certainly, hasn't happened to him yet.

September 24th, Overland Park, KS

Outside my office tower – a
couple times a day – I stand
under the sky in the world and smoke.

Today, the air is cool as
leaves on trees adjust to
the newly born season.

Cigarette smoke rises on breeze.

Maples redden, cottonwoods
gild, leaves – dressed
splendid – slip into the air
and surrender, quivering
throughout that short trip on
wind, to rest on grass,
cement, macadam, and dirt.
Soft light, autumn stained,
warms my shirt before I ascend
to climate control, open
cubicle, cluttered desk, email,
search engines, database
applications, fluorescent light,
cold coffee, and a telephone.

My Radiator Runneth Over

Wasted and wounded, it ain't what the moon did.
—Tom Waits

If a full harvest moon can affect the tides
pull water into waves
make us crazy
fill emergency rooms
take us out of our heads
then it is not too much to think
it is the reason why
Grace, my Buick of Destiny,
boiled forth green radiator froth
coming down a rain-soaked Mt. Mitchell
one hundred fifty miles from home
at night with me
flat broke.

Joel Explains Why My LeSabre Isn't Ready

Oh, hey Shawn.
I ain't really had a chance
to tear into 'er yet.
See, my machinist
done lopped 'e's thumb off
and he's a day behind.

Reclaiming the Light

Can't stop what's coming
can't stop what is on its way
—Tori Amos

The sun will come up,
come what may,
as you sit out there on the back porch
at 3 a.m. listening to the late-summer crickets
and the monotonic groan of
a secondhand window-unit air conditioner,
looking out through black shadows of leaves
over tops of low-rent houses
past skyscrapers
past the horizon and straight
into the center of what you cannot name,
a steaming, pumping mass
red and alive with the voice that haunts you,
a throatless voice ringing in your skull
raising you from your bed to sit
out there alone in your darkness,
in mid-September, long past midnight,
your heart pounding fast in the center of your chest
so you breathe & breathe & breathe
cool damp air
trying to clean the damage away,
trying to scour your blood, your heart, your head

of a voice that is your voice,
stronger when you are tired of fighting and smiling
through the darkness that greets you every day

so you light a match,
let your eyes adjust, and touch
that flame to the end of a cigarette
and inhale

ah yes, distraction,
light, a mantra in the dark
of light & ember & smoke

say it to yourself over & over & over
the sun will come up,
come what may,

again & again & again.

Monday Morning, 6:45 a.m.

Enormous and forested with whisper,
a flood of shadow smooths like water,
languid and cool, over rock,

and mists of knowing,
wiped away with sleep
from eyes of surfacing consciousness
boil away dark memories of beauty,
ethereal garden music,
lush with the sonorous tonality of
a translucent language of dream
evaporated from its liquid place
by early, practical, morning light.

Avoiding Traffic on the Morning Commute

One eye open
sipping drive-through coffee
two lanes filled with parked cars
at my exit to work.

With a quick rear-view glance
I gun the Mustang's engine, skirt the traffic
and take the next exit,
slow-boat my way down
side streets to the office.

It is a warm spring morning
as I pass a tractor-trailer
on my left, passenger-side window down,
a beagle with its head out in the wind
ears flapping, tongue lolling.

Best thing I'll see all day.

Turning 45

and the poets down here don't write nothing at all,
they just stand back and let it all be
—Bruce Springsteen

It's that feeling you get when you pull into the parking
lot at work in the morning listening to *Jungleland* just as
Clarence steps out for the saxophone bridge and your
heart just breaks
at the loneliness of it and you can remember
making music when you were younger
getting lost in the joy of it

but you can't open the goddamned car door
because you know

you just know
that this is the best your day will get

listening to The E Street Band
in the parking lot
of a fancy glass building
in a fancy office park before
trudging through automatic
doors and drinking weak
coffee and sitting in an open
cubicle breathing stale
air under fluorescent lights

while staring at a computer
screen dreading email
and telephones and making nice with people
with whom you share nothing but this.

It's that feeling.

Stunted Spring

Let a cold mist fall
on an early spring day
glazing a light covering of snow.
Quiet, except for a Kansas wind
battering trees in the backyard.
Listen and hear the winter's dead
limbs crack and crash into the hard earth
still rigid with cold and you will know
you are still in Kansas
and that winter is not done with you.
No, not with you.

Section III

*...Love is not
enough. We die and are put into the earth forever.
We should insist while there is still time.*

—Jack Gilbert

Little Big Star: for Alex Chilton (1950 – 2010)

I never travel far without a little Big Star
—Paul Westerberg

All that mattered was the song, Alex,
the letters and the words and
those succulent poppy hooks.

We danced for you, Alex, we learned
diminished chords for you. We bought your records
and played them on our turntables
until the vinyl wore so thin that light passed
through the grooves and it is that light we miss,
Alex, but it shines on wax and gleams in bright
binary code like the light we drank from you –

our Blue Moon in darkness – and it will
sustain us for now, Alex, until that next
misfit kid unsleeves *In the Street:*

without a thing to do
except talk to you.
Aah.

Dear Lucille: *on the passing of Lucille Clifton*
(1936 – 2010)

I would like to think that B.B. King
named his guitar for you. I know
he didn't. We in the know
know the myth, the real story –

we know that it is not you whom he
played to make music so sweet that I,
a grown man, cry when I hear it –

but I am comforted thinking it is so
even though you did not need a man for making music,
your wide hips spinning men like tops (we never doubted
it for a second!)

and your words spinning out to the sky
because the pages could not hold them
for long, Lucille, could not keep them
silent, all black and white

your words like you bigger than what they lay upon and
they echo like you now that you're gone
so that sadness cannot take hold for long, Lucille.

Thermodynamics: *for Luther Pavey*

The ground that bore him swallowed him whole,
between Christmas and New Years, my
father's father, dressed in a suit never worn
except for weddings and other funerals.

Around his unaccustomed neck, a tie. In
his trousers' pocket, a buckeye, small and
smooth, a piece of his earth. Ever present,
he would hold it in his hand, between his
palm and fingers, that fruit of immense
wooden possibilities.

And in his little corner of Indiana, on a hill overlooking
his house and the land he worked, near his father and
mother gone some fifty years, those who knew him
gathered to watch what he left behind
be lowered into dirt.

The mound of earth settles now. By the end of spring, it
will level. And in years, concave.
With luck, the buckeye will sprout from his hip, will
spread thick solid roots deep through his body, snap
casket walls, pull in soil. The roots will break brittle
bones and grind my granddad to dust.

And from the place of his long sleep a tree
will spring forth through sod, will grow tall,
will stretch into sky towards sun.

Years from now, I will come back to that grave to touch a
tree's rough bark, be shaded by its branches,
breathe oxygen from its leaves, and know as he knew, as
we all know, that energy
can neither be created nor destroyed.

Poem for Sara Romweber

You should have poems written for you
full of drum fills and cymbal crashes, poems
to your wild hair, to your fierce kindness.
You should have been able to read those poems
in a book, in *Rolling Stone,*
on the backs of record covers
in the cool stores where your friends worked.

I'm digging through old albums today,
blowing dust off so they will play
on one of these turntables still hooked up
to half decent speakers and a working receiver,
and it's been two days since you died

and in listening I hear thunder and chaos
from your kit but you were always in time.
Even your cancer had the word *blast* in it
but there are no poems here.
I only have this story and I tell it all the time:

Your band, Snatches of Pink,
opened for Jason and the Scorchers
at the Cat's Cradle in Carrboro. After your set,
you wandered into the crowd and I couldn't
resist the chance to tell you how great you sounded,

how you played your drums
like a shaped explosive charge,
how your rhythms soundtracked my life

and you thanked me and hugged me
with your whole face smiling like I was an old friend.
All I could do was blather on about who knows what
because Rock Star hugs
are such rare and disarming things.

It's been two days and all I can do
is write this poem
when it's too damned late
and hope that somebody, sometime,
wrote you a poem, too, and that you held
it in your strong, tiny hands.

I hope it made you smile.

Excerpt from *Ghosts on Water: A Kansas City Renga*

Stand on the corner
of 39th and Bell, the
ghosts of Victor Smith

and Phil Miller sing poems
of Kansas City and dust

to cars moving slow
through streets just spitting distance
from the borderline

and that other state, the one
blanketed in plains grass, dreams.

The World Is Small and Fragile Still:
for Scott Waldrup

A screen tells me without a single noise
as photo after photo of a sweet goofball
former student shows up in my Facebook feed

and it takes time to register,
I don't understand immediately,
and then, when I stop my mindless scrolling,

start to pay attention, read and pay attention,
suspicion emerges as fact
and that student lies in a morgue

after pushing people to safety last night
and shielding them with his now man's body
from a speeding sport utility vehicle

driven by another mass shooter
fleeing police pursuit
in Savannah, Georgia.

His young body, lying in a morgue,
silent on a slab, silent in a morgue.

Remembering: *for Bob Sheldon*

These nights pass in such long hours
Even moonlight seems so still
You can almost touch it.

Go ahead.
It won't bite.
Can't really hurt you.
Go ahead.

Time again to be alone.
No known comfort exists here before dawn
and radio is the only sound
save the humming of a digital alarm clock
progressed past ticking.

dead
Dead.

There, I've said it. Again.
But writing it down feels too much
like writing you off, brother,
no shit.

Memory fails to bring you into focus.
Only patches of image come through,
your voice the only constant I conjure,

your voice over warm sour-mash bourbon
belly-laughing like a kid
on the beat-up old couch
on your book store's front porch
before wandering out to catch a band
at a bar down the street
to dance.

And we knew we'd always dance with you,
but a lousy little bullet got in our way
and you, shot in your head,
are just ash spread over some mountain now.

I would welcome any sound –
a click, a tock –
some signal of passage
other than the silent movement of constellations
and a fractioned sphere past my window

so slow, I barely notice.

So slow, I sit alone in dark,
cigarettes my only light except hope
of a sun rolling up in the east.
Through my window, I'll see it,
knowing you can't.

Knowing you won't.

Love Letter to the World

Here, in this season of dying,
neighbors, three of them in as many years,
spouses and nephews and parents of co-workers,
playwrights, artists, poets, musicians, and actors,
old acquaintances and classmates and teachers
with whom I had not spoken in decades,
all of whom I adored,
friends and family so far from here;
this list growing longer through all of my days.

It is Sunday in eastern Kansas,
under a wide blue and temperate
summer sky, cool sweat on my brow
from a morning mow, I am wishing
I am wishing I am wishing and I wish
for all of us, all of us, more time
in back yards, on porch swings,
around barbecue grills, in living rooms,
in kitchens, in coffee shops, book stores, and bars.

Let us speak to each other
over cups in which we hold
our broken spirits together
where we sip our beer,
drink our coffee, hell, I'll even brew
strong sweet tea that we can
pour over ice with or without
fine bourbon on the side.

Let us talk of our lives together and separate,
speak softly of things
in our shattered and mended hearts,
tell such stories that weave us into a tapestry
of our larger, collected selves.

Find me here or there or wherever I may be.
Take my hand, grab my shoulder,
then let us steal away to a quiet corner
and enjoy some music or sit in silence,
together in this whole, big mess of a world.

Breakfast With Baldinger

As your lawyer, he starts,
*I recommend that you take the day
off from work. Start with edible marijuana
to take care of that hangover in spectacular fashion
and coat it all with French toast.
Play guitar for a while,
then spend the afternoon at the art museum.
Follow that with a spicy Bloody Mary and barbecue
for a late lunch. Swing by Prospero's
to shoot the shit with Tom.
Resist buying the beat-up hardcover
10-volume collection of the World's Greatest Poetry.
Retire to home to drink gin bucks
and watch Otis Rush play an Epiphone Riviera
upside down and left handed on DVD
in Dolby Surround Sound.*

Robert Johnson at the Crossroads

You've got to spin the bottle just so.
Put the right amount of hip check
and pool cue English on it.
Needs to be a night like this
where lightning just looks
for something to strike
and there's blood, of course,
from a knife cut deep
in the left palm meat.

Then, well, man, then
you just have to wait.

Think long and hard
on that thing you can't
live without anymore. For me,
it's this '28 Gibson. I swear
to God that some nights
she'll sing sweeter than
any bird you ever heard
but not every night, you know?
Not every night.

An old man with a shiny cane
takes the bottle with my blood
and drinks every goddamn drop,
licks his lips, and pulls some papers
out of his dark jacket pocket.

Now, you don't need to read that, son.
Just dip this pen into that cut.
You want to make your mark, now,
don't you?

Won't cost you anything you're using, anyway.

A Gift, So It Seems

Our short-hair tortoise shell,
tail at attention, paces insistently
in front of a tattered welcome mat,
presenting, in artful display,
her gift of meat:

a small, half-grown rabbit
opened from throat to belly,
head separated from spine
but still, somehow, attached.

Squeaking with delight, our huntress
bolts inside as I creak open
the screen door.

I give her a petting, fresh
water, some dry food,
and retrieve a grocery bag
which I invert to pick up
a soft, broken, still-warm body

and carry it to a tree
in the back yard to bury
next to all the others.

Auditioning for Heaven: *for Chuck Sullivan and M. Scott Douglass*

Blending into the constructed stage
our voices propelled poetry through the mic
through the P.A.
into the air
vibrating a uniting physics of molecular events
finding passerby ears finding
no interest

only humming bird buzzes of mosquito annoyance
metaphors attended to like a deaf man
to a dog whistle

rhythm and sound finding no ground
to take root
to hold words bouncing free
of substance in Independence Park

camouflaged by indifference
under a blue heaven stretching wide
over a Carolina Spring afternoon
where only God listens
to meter rolling out over 7th and Hawthorne
with tires of cars

headed someplace else.

Schizophrenia

His vampires are back again
rising up from hallucinatory mists
of madness gleaming at the edge
of group home rooms.

Nosferatu roommates,
demonic staff,
and steak knives from the dishwasher
become weapons slicing through monsters
on the way out the door.

Imagined blood is real enough

and state hospital beds possess thick leather straps
that bind bodies in place.
Screams never travel far past padded walls
where Thorazine is not holy water,
wooden stake,
or crucifix,

where shadows creep in through his eyes,
and nightmares linger when he wakes.

Jason Ryberg in the Gasconade

Here on a lazy Saturday, all things float
in a weightlessness known
only by swimmers and astronauts
deep between sand and rock and all that
lurks just beyond a rippled surface
of space and time.

Dogs luxuriate on a wooden deck
overlooking wide green currents
panting in Missouri's late summer heat,
gnawing at fleas.

Jason Ryberg steps into Gasconade waters
every day never touching the same river twice
which fosters a wondering
of which world greets us
in those first moments
of each pregnant day?

Is this when the bill is due?
Is this that day a new poem
slithers into some mystical space
between spinal chord
and cerebellum?
Is this that day? Is this that world?

Jason Ryberg emerges wet,

wanders to porch,
finds a beer hiding
in the back of the fridge
and cracks that fucker open
right then and there,
swallows a long pull,
and smiles.

Tapestry: *for Chuck Sullivan on his 60th Birthday*

Into every word you weave a poetry that drips the
language with color, slickens the long and short threads
of meaning with a juice all your own.
Almost twenty years ago you showed me new speech,
taught me new music, made ink dance for me to its own
funk drunk on the Irish whiskey of its art.
A thick football player, oboist, scribbler, misfit,
you took to me as if your own, gave to me
your light, the one that shines not on darkness
but being,
           illuminating all that is human – all
the songs of innocence and experience
resonating forth, twisting and spinning
through the eye of the needle through which

rich men cannot pass, sewing
together in God's grandeur
                        a tapestry that covers all of
us you touch spreading out such warmth
as the heart has no right to bear.

At the Waffle House

Behold, I show you a mystery;
we shall not all sleep
but we shall all be changed

—I Corinthians 15:51

Out of beer and out of time,
last call puts Tyler and me in a place
where mysterious blendings of caffeine and nicotine
work our Budweiser-dulled brains awake,
where redneck jukeboxes full of whiskey voices
lament great losses of the true ones
and how we all get stomped
flatter than lonely Texas highways
complete with tumbleweeds and dust devils
simply by love.

So where are the rest of those Hank Williams poets
whose tears fall to the ground like rain
making puddles only bleary-eyed drunks
drinking their way through their blues can see?

When thy cup is empty, it shall be filled.
When she gets around to it
and isn't bellowing side orders
of bacon with those hash browns.

So go ye then on down to a place
where things somehow come to short order
in those small hours before dawn
in fogs of conversation
rambling through coffee steam
and cigarettes piling dead in testament
to a new faith healing
busted hearts in confirmation
that you will never be the same.

Section IV

I bought a pack of Camels yesterday.
What do I care if World War III breaks out?
Whatever happens happens anyway.

—William Harmon

Story

I wish I could tell you
the story of the world,
how sun and moon
gained dominion
over day and night,
how land rose up
and sea settled low.

I would tell you how
stars were born, how
birds learned to dance in wind,
how fish breathe water, how
fire surges from spark.

I wish I could tell you
how man shed the animal inside,
but the story of the world shows
man, standing
on two legs, fists clenched;
inventing – first – blade,
not plow.

A Christmas Wish

A very merry Christmas
And a happy New Year
Let's hope it's a good one
Without any fear
—John Lennon

If He came back this season,
rising from Bethlehem
filled with divine purpose,
Jesus would build an army.

Tall, carpenter strong, sunburned still
from those three days in the desert
on the cross,
His sun-streaked flowing locks buzz cut
and razor sharp now,
He would march out in front of
His army of saints and angels and important people
like Gandhi. Dr. King. The Buddha. Mohammed. Lao
Tzu. Malcolm X. And Ben Franklin,
all pudgy and bespectacled.
I think He'd bring Nelson Mandela with him.
Socrates. Sure. Why not?
Hell, He might even bring back Nietzsche
just to fuck with him.

George Harrison (he's always got such great pot).
Immanuel Kant to teach us ethics.
Jonas Salk and Eleanor Roosevelt and Mother Theresa
and Princess Di to help care for the wounded
and the maimed and the orphaned and the dead.
I think Jimmy Carter would be in Jesus' army
to build houses for the homeless,
Woody Guthrie and Pete Seeger and Leadbelly
would sing to empower the workers.
Langston Hughes would teach us all to dream.
Frank Lloyd Wright and Leonardo DaVinci
could help draw up the plans to rebuild the world.
Jerry Falwell would be back
to take out garbage and dig latrines and shovel shit.

Jesus would lead His army out over the whole Earth.
But Jesus would not be welcomed.
Bullets and missiles and bombs
would be fired at Him,
IEDs would be set in His path.

All would be ineffective.
Bullets would become bread. Missiles, medicine. Bombs
would build hospitals.
IEDs would build schools.
RPGs become clean water to drink.
He would take the blood-thirsty
and the enraged and the misguided

and hold them in the warm embrace of His love,
of Allah's love, of Buddha's peace,
and the Tao's wisdom.

He would go to Baghdad and Faluja,
Tora Bora and Kabul,
Chechnya, Kosovo, Darfur, Mauritania, Jerusalem,
Palestine, Liberia, Ethiopia, Myanmar, Syria, Lebanon,
Ghana, Haiti, Somalia, the Ukraine, Christchurch.
Newtown, San Bernadino, Ferguson. Baltimore,
Orlando, Charleston, Las Vegas, Littleton, Parkland,
Dallas, New York.
He would go to all the bloody places in the world
and heal shattered bodies, broken hearts,
poisoned minds.

Netanyahu would bow to Him,
Hamas would dismantle their suicide bombs,
the Islamic State would tweet their surrender.
Al Qaeda would lay down their Kalashnikovs
come down from the mountains to know peace.
They would know that this Jesus is a man
who died once nailed to boards on a hot hill
and would do it again
and how does one kill what does not die?

Marching East from Israel,
China would take notice

and hold free and open elections,
encourage dissent, apologize to the Dalai Lama,
and withdraw from Tibet.

Sworn enemies would fall on their knees, weeping,
feeling in the center of all that they are
that this thing that Jesus has done
has changed them, made them see, finally,
that killing for an idea kills that very idea every time.

By now, Jesus is more than Himself.
More than the punisher that Paul
the Epistler made Him.
More than the political tool
that Emperor Constantine envisioned.
Now, Jesus is reason.
He is kindness and compassion and fairness.
He has shed the vanity
and no longer needs capital letters to describe him.
He is the divine within all of us.
He is the best that we can be.

He will go, *en masse,* to America,
start on the West Coast, spread his Army
(which by now has grown to include all peoples
from the rest of the world)
throughout the land,
which has finally become our land.

Drought-stricken farms will flourish,
the poor and hungry will eat.
People needing work will find jobs
paying fair wages for their toil.
CEOs will leave their leather chairs
for the assembly lines.
The working poor will have time
to be with their children.
Everyone will read. Cars will run on water.
Water will be clean enough to drink.
Ice caps will refreeze.
Wildlife will thrive
and Johnny Weissmuller will be there with Jesus,
yodeling and swinging on vines,
protecting the animals from harm.
Advertisers will stop selling
diet aids and beauty creams.
Cigarettes will no longer look cool.
Malt liquor and fast food
will no longer be marketed to the poor.
We will no longer feel the need to own too much.
We will work only to live.

Jesus will march his army east, to Washington.
The Marines, the Army, the National Guard,
the Air Force, the Navy, the Coast Guard,
the Secret Service, the INS, the CIA, the FBI,
the NSA, Homeland Security,

the FDA, the CDC, the GOP, the Skull and Bones,
the Salvation Army, the Moral Majority,
the Focus on Families, the 700 Club, the Rotary Club,
all will let him pass. Jesus has become
more than any of them can handle.

The Pentagon will be converted to low cost housing
because Jesus, by this time, has made war
and the very idea of war stupid.
Everybody in the world agrees.

And Jesus will stop being Jesus.

He will fade away in front of us and become nothing
because this peace and this answer
lay inside us all along.
To be good, to do good,
that is enough and we all know it.
We do not need a god to fear.
Fear is why we failed for all of human time.

There will be great dancing Hindu celebrations
of life and of living.
Sufis will whirl in wild dervishes.
Native Americans will sing and dance
to their ancestors' drums.
Jews and Christians and Muslims shimmy and shake,
side by side, to klezmer music.

Hava Nageela means *Let's Rejoice*. Indeed! Let's!
All the peoples of all the world will dance
because now, finally, there is joy in the world
and *angels we have heard on high*
will sing *sweetly o'er the plain*
and the mountains in reply
will echo *their joyous strain.*

Gloria, we will sing,
in excelsis deo.

Ignoring the Homeless Man at the Corner of Johnson and Antioch, Then Meeting His Eyes

I drive a blue Mustang that shines in the sun.
It costs me and I pay for it,
but I'm almost free of the bank.

Friday evening, end of March,
long week at work, I took Johnson Drive
off the interstate
to stop at the pharmacy
for a prescription for my arthritic knees.
At the red light at Antioch, I stopped
behind a plumber's truck.

He is thin, this man standing in grass
on the corner holding a sign stating

The
Struggle
Is Real

I try not to see him. I had cash on me,
that's not the problem.

I've been scammed, sure. The guy in Charlotte
with the van out of gas. There was no van, no wife,
but I gave my last $20. The veteran in Louisville with the
hospital stay and his car in impound. The kids in

Midtown Manhattan who cleaned us out for donations
for their studio time. And, I'm sure,
everyone I've ever handed money to on the street.
I used to hand it out all the time, if I had any.

This guy, gaunt, bundled against
the still cold Kansas wind:

The
Struggle
Is Real

And I know this. I know it in every cell that I am.
I'm headed for arthritis medication, for Christ's sake.
I gave a car back to the bank once.
Been eight dollars away
from being this guy.

So, I pretend I don't see him
but can't stop looking
and we lock eyes in that way
you lock eyes with someone in pain

but I look away
as the light changes
and I hated that truck
in front of me
because I can't get out of there

fast enough
and I hate feeling ashamed.

Crossing the Street

I don't come to this corner too often.
Take the back streets and alley to the shelter.
Can't stand to see all them cars, man.
Used to sleep in mine till the bank found me.

I'd had a good day.
Made ten bucks raking an old lady's leaves.
Bought a burger and a pack of Marlboros.
Not them nasty-ass budget brand smokes, man,
but Marlboros.

Left them on the dash
when the repo boys yanked me out and beat me silly.
Took my Plymouth, my coat, and my smokes.

I mean, Jesus, if I could find a job
I'd get me one.
All I know is laying brick.
All them jobs is filled.
When folks stop building, brick layers get hungry.
And cold.
And when a man loses his car, well, it's pretty damned tough
to find work
or get to it.

The shelter's not so bad.
Three squares and a place to sleep.
I help out washing dishes and scrubbing toilets.

Don't ever take a handout,
that's what my daddy told me.
He shined shoes in the thirties
on Park Avenue in New York goddamned City
for a nickel a pop.
Paid for a room without heat
and cans of pork 'n' beans he ate cold.

But all I want to do anymore is just make it
across the street
dodging all them shiny cars
with people staring at me,
my dirty clothes, my dirty face.
I know I look like shit and smell like it, too.

A man never quite gets over
the smell of his own stink.

God Is on His Way

Just got a text from the Almighty.
He's running a little behind.
He was on his way to your subdivision
to bless you in your five-bedroom,
three-bathroom abundance because
you are so much in need of divine grace.

Anyway, the heavenly El Camino picked up
a bolt off the road in the sidewall
of the driver's side rear Firestone
because of all that highway
construction on Interstate 35
and, wouldn't you know it, his spare was flat, too.

He called triple A and is just waiting
for the tow truck.
Oh, he said to tell you that you'll be fine
but you should have figured that out by now
with your health insurance and 401k balance.

He also mentioned he can't stay long.
Something about Aleppo.

Lament in the Key of 4G

Out here in the Heartland, wind howls
hot across browning grass and concrete and cars.
We lose our voices; lose the sound of words
we use when shouting above the din of our lives.

Nothing provides comfort, so needed here –
this loud life.
                So much to remember.
We carry expensive dig-
ital phones to track our appointments,
send our truncated messages in dig-
angelic text, take our calls, give us
direction so we are never lost wherever

we are and wherever we
go we never escape; noise follows footsteps
and driving and spending and
                        working and working and working.

Getting Away

Summer, and a fierce heat
bakes Midwest dirt into
cracked hardtack.

Longing for a hot season stain, water calls us
with its fluid surf, cool splash, breaking wave
relief from it all – the jobs and the traffic and
the choking bumper-to-bumper stink of it all.

Just want a cold drink on the hot sand.

In our fantasy, it's all white
beaches and iced beer coolers,
not balls of putrid tar, not fetid
petroleum stench, not
blackened dead wild things.
We want the cocoa butter smell
of it all, the sex and the sun of it all,
the hot-rod red convertible '58
Corvette of it all,
that green sea, that salt mist,
from memory and movies
and every picture postcard
from the Gulf

bought for loose change
at a gas station
off the interstate.

Hollow Point

Because bullets don't kill well enough
manufacturers hollow them
to blossom in penetrated flesh
even though last night
10 police officers and two civilians
were shot in Dallas
where five officers died
and the day before, two black men
were shot to death by police officers
on video live-streamed to everyone
and even though 100 people in Orlando
were shot while dancing last month
and poor little Tamir Rice
and Trayvon Martin
and Michael Brown
and all the names and all the names
and all the names this poem could be filled with
from Sandy Hook San Bernardino Charleston
Littleton Columbine Ft. Hood Parkland
names of innocents
whose places at dinner tables across America
are empty and empty rooms of soldiers
killed so far from home
and empty beds in Pakistan Afghanistan Libya
Syria Iraq Palestine Chechnya Serbia Croatia
all these names a hollow poem

its endless reams of pages on pages
written in blood that never dries
and is never enough to fill
all the hollow points
hollowing bleeding bodies
these hallowed bodies of the dead

Meme Language Poem

He cannot even. He cannot even, does not believe,
misspells *fact* as "F-A-K-E."
Donald Trump cannot even with journalism,
with science, with Constitution,
with checks and balances,
oh, he cannot even with rule of law.

Donald Trump likes women on their knees
but not black men in shoulder pads on their knees,
but not sneakers or cleats or sweatshirts
with a swoosh for a label.
He cannot even with black men and brown men.
Black women and brown women.
Black children and brown children.
Donald Trump cannot even,
not with black and brown.

Donald Trump sees good people on both sides,
he sees good people on the Nazi side
he sees good people on the Klan side
he forgets about my grandfather's blood
on an overgrown battlefield in France
he doesn't see Nazi shrapnel in his knees.

Donald Trump cannot even
America, America.

How to Keep a Fairy Down:
after a photo by Timm Wherry

Put her on a street in any no count
nothing special American town
don't give her an education
let her shackle herself
to 25 years of student loan debt
or better yet
let her try to get a job
flipping burgers or packing meat
or cleaning McMansions or industrial parks
without any language skills
or citizenship documentation
let her try to feed her winged sprite family
on what she can earn or just put her
on the street with a hopeful fairy hand
outstretched to strangers for a little kindness
a little love a little compassion a little cash
to blow fresh wind beneath her bright wings.

Survival Tips for the Pending Apocalypse

Know this: you can survive
on a diet of red beans and rice indefinitely.
Just stock the basement with cases of Texas
Pete Hot Sauce. Plant cabbage and carrots now
for cole slaw because you can't descend
into full-blown goddamned savagery just yet.
Let some of that garden go to seed and store it all
in a cool, dry space for next year. Load up the larder
with as much white vinegar, vegetable oil,
and black peppercorns as it can hold
because you just can't trust mayonnaise.
You can crack a peppercorn with a hammer
if the peppermill gives out. Oh.
Stock up on hammers.

Acquire a rooster and some hens
for the back yard and fence that fucker off
high and tight. Don't be cheap with
the razor wire, which can be found at any
black site CIA prison or bad neighborhood
title loan shop for next to nothing. Chicken
is good, man, even when the rest of the world ain't.

Lay in as much cracked corn animal feed
as you can find because chickens got to eat, too,
but save some for yourself
in case you find yourself in a pinch.

Stock up on ten-penny nails
and hundred-dollar bourbon:

nails to fix the shit you know will break
and bourbon to fix the shit you can't.

Get used to drinking hundred-dollar bourbon.

Section V

Poetry is not only a dream and vision; it is the skeleton architecture of our lives. It lays the foundations for a future of change, a bridge across our fears of what has never been before.

—Audre Lorde

A Bluesman's Guide to Eastern Religion

If you meet the Buddha on the road,
take him to a juke joint and get him drunk.
Play him old Muddy Waters records and ask him
if nirvana can really be found in the head of this,
his next beer.

Rumbling Through Dreams

I.

At midnight and two, it shook walls
with a diesel and steel roar
that could wake the deaf,
yet in a little house built next to tracks,
my brother and I,
stacked in bunk beds,
slept a practiced sleep
as the Burlington Northern rumbled west
through our dreams.

II.

Walking in measured steps
from crosstie to crosstie,
I followed that line,
eyes forever to the horizon,
never losing sight of the point
where it all comes together,
stopping only to mine the best pieces of rose quartz,
mica, and coal,
from beside the tracks.

When a train would come, off in the distance,
before moving clear,
like in the movies, I put my ear
to the rail just to hear
the music of steel rolling over steel.

And, at the end of the day,
all walked out,
I dropped my treasure in a tattered sneakers box
with collected stamps, Bicentennial quarters,
Apache tears, and letters from grandparents
half a continent away.

III.

In the mornings before breakfast
in arid Colorado summers,
I ran to the tracks,
to the special place on the rail
where I put pennies the night before,
smoothed flat by impact and mass
of trains carrying coal from the mountains,
sugar beets from the eastern plains,
delighting in the occasional remnant of Lincoln –
a nose, an ear, an eye, a texture of beard,
an *e pluribus unum*,
each atom of currency destroyed each a different way.

IV.

I dream of riding trains,
of winding serpentine
through the American patchwork.
East Coast forests blending
into Great Plains wheat,
rolling Ohio hills flattening
into the Kansas horizon
slamming into the sheer granite faces
of Rocky Mountain cliffs
and then, through desert sand,
to the sea.

I dream of salt mist and factory smoke,
ponderosa pine and sequoia,
of rain-pelted windows and thick valley fog.
I dream, and in my dreams, I ride trains
and do not make good time
but rather ride forever on trains that never stop,
longing to reach the place just ahead,
the elusive point of perspective
where the rails merge,
where the separate become singular,
where all things bind together
to be the one thing: whole.

Thaw

In winter, the body knows
it is born to vanish.

Flesh turns to dirt, bones wash white
in March rains.
Life churns, returning
to wet layers of earth.

We – dead and dying, rotten and rotting –
look up to a sun far away and wait,
wait for the body and the solar body
to pull each other closer,
moisten skin with sweat,
heat blood,
crack seeds,
green the dead husk of the world.

In spring, the body knows
it is born to sing.

Leonid Meteor Shower With James

I.

Our bodies clothed against air cold
                enough to freeze water where it stands,
James and I stand and look skyward,
    to the northwest,

        sipping coffee in the dark of our yard.

Crazy enough, we two,
                to watch rock burn in the sky
          as the matter and the atoms of the matter
break down,
        component parts reassembling
into something altogether new.

II.

This, we will not see again.
                90 years will pass.
We will not see
      this rain of rock
of fire   of ash

mingling with the air we breathe.

        We will not taste on our tongues burning
     sky, crackling energy, as steam
from our breath swirls a silvered
        motion away from our bundled-up selves.

Big as fists, big as elephants' heads, as small
as a grain of sand,
     meteors

sizzled dark sky two hours before dawn
November's July 4th fireworks
raining bright fire
              down on us,
incandescent particles
     exploding into air connecting us
     to all that is in
              this infinite expanse
where we spin in perfect symmetry.

III.

     90 years will pass,
politicians will die.
Captains of industry   will die.
Priests   will die.

And monks.

   And James.
     And me.

Before meteors meet us again,
lighting a dark night with embers,
   we will all die.

IV.

   Bringing fire,
meteors will shimmer a dark sky,

they will pour upon the earth,
    spread dusts from places we have not seen,

they will come again
   out of darkness as before

when the world still steamed in the chill
       from its new birth.

They will bring with them
fire, a breath they will breathe
     into bones and dust and ash,

   they will breathe into the air, stain the sea,
vapor into clouds a fresh mattering.

Who will stand in the cold dark then?
Who will smell the fire in the night?

Will they coat themselves against frost and ice,
drink the black
   coffee of morning before light,
will they delight in a spectacle of fiery mists,

      will they fix their eyes on heaven?

Modern Alchemy

Keeping eyeglasses clean. Choosing the right tax preparation software. Voting for local judges. Deciphering Chinese assembly instructions. Reading nutrition labels. Finding a good sneaker in a 13 wide. Folding fitted sheets. Writing a good poem.

Morning

It is a simple act,
the brewing of coffee in the chill
of a dark March morning.

My cheap automatic drip machine
belches and spits a grotesque sound
as pleasing as any cello concerto
or crow squawk,
making music to make me wake.

The sun will rise soon.

This sky will move from black to gray
and from the window of this low-rent,
one-bedroom apartment
I'll see the three-story side of Queen City
TV & Appliance,
its top to bottom cracked wall anointed
with a healing concrete salve and stitched up
by two iron bars bolted into brick.

But now it is only a black slab in invisible decay
in the shadows of new monuments
straining up from downtown Charlotte streets,
scratching at the horizon
with jagged spires of steel and glass
shiny like aluminum foil crowns
littering the sky like a playground.

Cars already begin to sputter by on the streets below.

A block away to the West,
an ambulance siren screams,
dopplering around a corner.
Buses will soon lumber by
with their high-pitched diesel moans and sighs,
short sharp squeals of air-brake expulsions.

Ceiling creakings above me signify movement,
an unknown body staggering
into the consciousness of another day.
It is business as usual:
a toilet flush,
a cascading of pressure-fed water through
a shower nozzle
bouncing off a metal tub.

The sun has risen, silently.

I somehow always expect to hear it creak and groan
in the well-worn motions of a task
so ancient and lasting
that maybe we don't even notice the sounds;
the universe itself being such a well-oiled,
well-maintained cog works,
its machinations leaving us in a silence
we don't even notice our noisy bumblings
through the days and nights of our own movement.

And remarkable even yet is the singing of birds,
pigeons and robins,
dingy with the dusts of city living.
Early morning light finds them perched
on power lines through which the juice
of coffee makers and electric alarm clocks
flows in turbine-generated currents.

The brick wall through my window begins to glow
as only orange and red cooked clay can,
vibrant and dull.

Coffee has brewed and I sip it slowly in new light
where somewhere away from this city
dogwood trees bloom fragrant, crucifix blossoms
and finches and towhees may sing sweeter songs
than the awkward soundings
of mockingbirds on telephone lines
in the center of a rumbling city

yawning and cursing itself awake.

Excerpt from *Radio Renga for KKFI*

To start, it vibrates our cochlear bones, those living cones, that funnel sound to wet, gray brains as waves oscillate through sky – in a frequency

of deep longing, moving body and blood in such funk that it whisks us down, down through time, to a moment when radio becomes a thing of our own, at night, through headphones as parents think we sleep. A distant station strums our dreams. Can't you hear it? Can't you just hear it now?

Manifesto No. 132

Light ignites a maple leaf
in just such a way each autumn.

Guitars buzz deep in
bones and eardrums.

A lover's wink
inflates a chest
to bursting.

These things bring a man to stand,
to say out loud at once

I am alive right
here now. In this place.

I am here, alive,
homunculus in all
space and all time.
These are my footsteps
and this is my breath
misting in October night.

It matters. It has to.

Architecture

*Grisly, foul, and terrific
is the speech of bones*
—Donald Hall

Brittle and dry,
white and empty
of marrow – bones
cook in a desert sun.

Molecules in the heat
crack wide open,
atoms spill out onto sand
a fine powder once alive.

Vestige of frame,
purpose of structure,
crumbles and flakes
layer after layer.

Over what was once *coyote,* wind
thunders through skull cavities,
howls a *vox phasmatis.*

Homecoming

An iridescent film of bacterial radiance
glowed green on the Atlantic
under a luminous straining of new day sun

and whispered wind music
sang over waves snaking froth
massaging the sand
washing in time with a morning tide
the feather script of an unwritten poem
scrawled in a language of emerging light
sea strained against the edges of itself
rippling water beneath a mottled cumulus sky
throbbing an ancient fluid melody

and with my white toes in the surf
an ocean of first water
ebbed saline over my skin

pulsed like blood.

Analysis: *after Jonathan Swift*

Take a '57 Chevy
completely apart
and just try to call it a car.

Go ahead.
Pick up any damned piece you want.

A disassembled carburetor lying next to a dis-
embodied distributor cap will still
be separated from any sense of street legality.

But put it back together
and it will take you
where you want to go
in style.

So, break a poem down, I mean all the way down,
and all you are ever going to get
are lines of ink on glue-bound wood pulp
and where is the magic in that?

Just swallow it whole,
a thing like any other.
It will sit in your gut like a crank case.

Let gastric acids work on it as they will
and the atoms of the matter
reveal themselves in ways so mysterious
that you never forget what it does to you.

Inaudible Song

The Earth has music for those who listen.
—Reginald Vincent Holmes

Cafeteria choir lifts up its voice
in vacant chant without specific coherence,
the purest music of any communication.

Next time you lie awake,
sheets wrapped violently from twist and turn –
car horns will blow a defective F,
dogs respond,
street lights hum without breath,
and tires on rain-slick pavement sing hushed songs.

Surrounded by sound since the amniotic daze,
we witness
particles oscillating in such noise
that we hear only the part we hear,
theme and vibrations of the physics
that binds us all to every other thing.

Soundproof

I read about a soundproofed room
so silent that no person lasted
more than 45 minutes within it,

a silence so complete that internal
psychologies break down.

It starts with an awareness of breath.
Ears ring. Blood pulses, pulses in veins.
Heart pumps its thud and thunder.
Muscles slip noisily about under skin.
Food gurgles through the digestive tract.
Joints creak and grind, creak and grind.
Then, hallucinations.

Without data, the mind makes its own.

Tread Marks on Mars

So cold there, and dry.
Scientists know this, know it from
data transmitted on radio waves from
bits of metal and plastic blasted into
space, hurtled to Mars.
Hurled like so many stones
at abandoned shack windows.
Hurled by children wanting a sound of shattering.

Air is thin but there is wind enough to brush tread
imprints in red dust bare, in time.

How strange the hum of electric servos must
sound whirring in such thin atmosphere, how drill bits
eating old stone squeal finding traces of water.

Could be there were ponds of it,
rivers of it. Seas.

There, now, sky just leaks away and
we are there watching from here
this heating, warring earth.

Ladder to the Moon: *after a painting by Georgia O'Keeffe*

When it's time, you'll know.
You'll see it hanging in front of you
as if it had always been there,
a handmade wooden ladder
above night-blackened red desert hills,
its bottom rung too high to even jump for,
top rung reaching nothing
save the space between earth sand and moon soil.

And somewhere past this desert,
past every thing,
strains a music of cinder blocks,
choirs of cranes and car horns,
and towers in New York reverberating a struggle
to reach only higher than they can.

If you can just see what is here,
then maybe a ladder will fall within your reach,
maybe it will carry you up
to touch and stand on a moon of your own,
to look down on towers of concrete, steel, and glass

that seem so small from there.

The Planets: *after Gustav Holst*

I.

Melody press, pound, make your way
as bullets, guns, blades re-sound screams.
World War One's not yet begun
and Mars' madness has to wait
for movements of sidereal significance
as Europe crumbles and soldiers march
through mud, blood, and battle gore.
Melody slips, fades, pounds away.

II.

Venus sings venereal songs
as spring deceives, piece by peace,
warm as winter's aftermath.
Her seasonal verse bud universal
harmony like lilacs and lilies
lifting themselves into the light.

III.

Swift Mercury, run the
vivace race.
Winged feet can tread no ground
and messages cannot wait.

IV.

Jovial Jupiter jests incessantly.
Where's the folly in being jolly?
Bound to earth by the gravity of our mass,
what he finds humorous never seems to humor us.
Thus, we fall, heels over head,
punchlined by jokes we just don't get.

V.

Bringer of old age, master of decay,
Saturn gives us bodies that wither.
From dawn to dead we dead and dying
trudge through autumn leaves that rot
and smell of eventual senility
as crumbling buildings smell like boiled things.

VI.

Gustav knew his magic well,
but Uranus knew it so much better
that Gustav heard the soldiers' boots
but could not see them marching
on their way to war and this one,
to end all others,
was just the beginning of another.

VII.

Neptune's mystic mist forms around us
as misunderstanding come so completely
that questions answered breed new questions,
new nuances before unknown, unnoticed.
The mystical we know we cannot know,
Its mystery slips our strongest grips,
and we, confused, fuse real with unreal,
blending enigmas into obvious fogs
we rarely venture to escape.

Finding Zen in Cow Town

In Kansas City's Union Station,
monks gathered to shake
colored sand that would become not sand,
but *Mandala*.

And here – pay attention now –
here is where it gets interesting:
a boy of three, maybe four,
saunters under the cordons
to do a little soft shoe
while monks ate, one assumes,
a simple meal.

Intricate designs and sharp, colored lines –
some no wider than a single small grain –
became the dust and scuffle
of a child's wilding abandon.

When asked, on the news that night,
what he thought of the security footage
of the child's sand dancing, of the mother's
quick grab and fast retreat, a monk replied, smiling,
We swept it up and started over.
We will just have to work faster now.

In a few days, in an unveiling ceremony,
attendees marveled
ooh and *ahh*.

And after all the cameras were packed away,
monks swept the second attempt
into a sacred vessel and poured it
into the waters of the Missouri
for good fortune.

The mandala, you see, is like this poem
that we find ourselves in this very moment;
the letters of each word, a grain of colored sand.
Dance in it, kick it around under
the soles of your feet.
Sweep it up.
Pour it in the river.

Let it all wash out to sea.

The Last Lunar Eclipse of the Millennium

*Looks like a yellow biscuit of a buttery cue ball moon
rolling maverick across an obsidian sky.*
—Tom Waits

Standing in bare feet
on an early autumn Carolina lawn,
my dew-slick skin
touched the new-mown grass, the moist soil
of the very earth whose shadow
can eclipse a moon

and a mythic Chinese moon-eating beast
gobbled Luna whole leaving only
a faint orange after-image
burning a shadow of flame
falling down on all of us
before the edge glowed
in silver white and blue
again, in time

filling a hole in the sky as big as life,
as big as all this.

Dissonance, Late August

Larval husks litter the fence
hang from tree bark and porch railings
discarded amber of the earth
from which they emerged after 17 years
of gnawing roots of trees
to unfurl gossamer wings, to fly

In evenings after work these last few weeks
I shut off the engine and open my car door
to a sound loud enough to stop thought
like fire alarms in office towers
and stare into the canopy of old trees
around my old house, my bad eyes
unable to make out their shapes
against the summer green of silver maple
and sweet gum leaves

singing and mating and trenching tree bark,
laying eggs, setting up a world
for their children who will hatch
to migrate with gravity into cool soil
and burrow deep to eat and sleep
and wait and wait and wait

The dying fall as we all will

Entertaining Equilibrium

I.

While drinking white wine yesterday
at a café down the road, I watched
the only waitress in the place
pile bus tubs as high as dirty dishes allowed
to dash through a maze of tables, chairs,
and the few remaining 3 o'clock patrons.

No utensil fell –
no clink, clank, or racket –
on her way to the kitchen.

One bad foot would have sent her
hard enough into any obstacle
to send dishes flying.

II.

Living alone as I do is an old balancing act,
the trick with plates spinning on poles
long as broomsticks
to delight and amaze the toughest audience.

But let an unexpected breath
tip it out of symmetry and

I'll hold breath to compensate
lest the whole shebang come crashing
down around my skull,
scattering shattered pieces all over.

III.

Occasional movement corrects deficiencies,
the winding of spring-powered watches
whose hour hands never seem to move
past the mark, yet, none the less, do.

Divinity manifests itself in two hands and a face,
and banded to an arm, time never abandons a body
unless removed, or the winding neglected,
causing the faster hand to slow and still,
not moving past the minute stopped.

We try to bring ourselves into an order of things,
but things go on as usual.
If, given a fabricated click,
the measured survives the measuring,
and if you take out tick-tocking,
then time outlives Timex,
quartz crystals, sand, and
where is the balance in that?

Eagle Landing: *for the astronauts of Apollo 11*

That unrestrained spire riding
Olympic flames of science and prayer
landed two men on land
never before holding a weight of man
all those miles above the very sky itself:
Apollo's flaming chariot bearing no gods
but men armored in suits crafted by hands
that never escaped the earth
except only in dreams or in death.

And wasn't death the risk
that three faced before,
that fourteen others faced after,
that escaping the surly bonds of this mass
on which all of us must always walk
save the twelve who strolled on lunar soil
somehow defies nature's numerical sense
of the unwritten laws even Icarus
could not escape.

I was only two
when that single white needle of 36 stories
but so much more than even that
stuck ghostly in my brain
with black and white memory

propelling me later to view
the silver face of the moon
through a white cardboard telescope
lying in summer nights on Colorado lawn
praying the deepest prayer
a ten-year-old could muster
to get a closer look,
oh, please God, let it be so

to drift only later into dreams
of silver darts shooting past the sky,
dreams as sacred as prayers
that even now I pray

as hard as any boy ever could.

Listening: an excerpt from *To the Stars through Difficulty: A Kansas Renga*

Listening: how wheat
bristles in wind like tele-
graph wires charged with part-

icles carrying voices
of dark communications

deeper than music
of our bright songbirds. Seeds of
prairie grasses crack

secret in the loam, yearn for
wildfires of blanketing shoots.

Tempus Fugue

Do I dare disturb the universe?
In a minute there is time
For decisions and revisions which a minute will reverse.
—T.S. Eliot

And on the moonlit sundial on Morehead planetarium's lawn
we lay right down you and me
accompanied by trumpets of breeze moving the flesh
of raven leaves resonating eternal rhythms
of chlorophyll-filled veins
stiffened toward stars in prayer
in the center of all things born and dead and unborn
echoing at once
a symphony of spheres staining the night in a resolute
paradox of existence and non-existence
light and dark
all time and no time without time to measure

and we
drunk on complexity's thick nectar
of chaos and order
bound to all things here and there
now and forever
then and never
by grace
became travelers in time and space
grasping at the impossibility of moments just passed

giddy like children
when at that moment a camera
would have captured us static on our backs
lying in the middle of the round ball of all time
your tiny slender fingers woven into mine
creating a single connection
on a dial unlit by sun
calculating nothing
as two dark bodies at rest stared
pupils wide
up to where explanation finds only mystery
and God balancing
now and never
then and forever
amen.

Shawn Pavey has delivered newspapers, mowed lawns, bagged groceries, cut meat, laid sewer pipe, bussed tables, washed dishes, roofed houses, crunched numbers, rented cars, worked in hotels, worn an apron at Kinko's, and been paid to write everything from résumés to music reviews. Currently, he earns a living as an Executive Recruiter in Mission, KS where he lives with his wife and two worthless but adorable cats. He is the author of *Talking to Shadows* (2008, Main Street Rag Press) and *Nobody Steals the Towels from a Motel 6* (2015, Spartan Press), Co-founder and former Associate Editor of *The Main Street Rag Literary Journal*, and a former board member and officer of The Writers Place, a Kansas City-based literary non-profit. His poems, essays, and journalism appear in a variety of national and regional publications. He's hosted poetry readings in bars, coffee shops, haunted houses, bookstores, libraries, front porches, seedy motel rooms, and abandoned warehouses. A graduate of the University of North Carolina's Undergraduate Honors Creative Writing Program, he likes his Tom Waits loud, his bourbon single-barrel, and his basketball Carolina Blue.

www.ingramcontent.com/pod-product-compliance
Lightning Source LLC
Chambersburg PA
CBHW030117100526
44591CB00009B/427